# GREAT QUESTION

Generating Effective Questions for
Successful Outcomes

by Doug Collins

ISBN: 978-0-9854374-5-9

*Other Books by Doug Collins:*

- The Dirty Maple Flooring Company Enters the Digital Age
- Innovation Architecture™ Volume 2: A New Blueprint for Engaging People through Collaborative Innovation
- Innovation Architecture™ Volume 1: A New Blueprint for Engaging People through Collaborative Innovation

*To Sheila and Arevik.*

———————●———————

*The answers to some questions
lead to joy.*

"Always the beautiful answer who asks a more beautiful question."
— E. E. Cummings

GREAT QUESTION!

## Preface

Several years ago I was working with the technology team supporting a very large player in the consumer packaged goods industry.

This group was focused internally on how they might pursue collaborative innovation in order to serve their brand clients with more compelling insights. Our engagement was at the time when companies began taking big data seriously.

**"It is not that I'm so smart. But I stay with the questions much longer."**

**—Albert Einstein**

The group consisted of smart, experienced people. Yet, as sometimes happens, they struggled with why they were there. What might they accomplish together?

At one point, the leader of the group—who herself consulted with the company's CEO—turned to me and, in a moment of admirable candor, observed, "We are not very good at asking ourselves questions, are we?"

Her reflection stuck with me. It serves as the inspiration for this book.

My first reaction was to think, simply, "Yes—this group is struggling."

Why do so many people struggle to identify and articulate the question that seemingly is top of mind? The question, which, if asked, might lead to real transformation?

There could be many reasons for this—demands on our time and the pressure to get things done, the natural tendency to leap to a solution assuming we know the problem or, back in school, the problem was a given and we spent most of our time on solving it.

Regardless of the reason, too often we don't devote enough time and attention to defining the problem or challenge question for ideation.

This small book, then, is for the leader of a group of people who would like to help guide that group in forming effective challenge questions for the purposes of generating ideas for innovation, collaboration and problem solving.

What question, were we to pursue it together, might lead to authentic breakthroughs?

My intent is that the leader reads through this book and, from a small investment in time, achieves better results.

I welcome your perspective on this topic and on the book, proper.

Email me at **doug.collins@innovationarchitecture.com**.

## Introduction

We hear, "there is no such thing as a bad question."

While we can appreciate the spirit that informs that statement, we can see, however, that there is such a thing as a question that misses the point, that leads the witness, or that confuses people.

These questions neither engage nor inspire us. They leave us scratching our heads, or worse, uninterested.

> "In all my affairs it's a healthy thing now and then to hang a question mark on the things you have long taken for granted."
> — Bertrand Russell

The purpose of this book is to help you as the leader of a business, group, program, or initiative ask better questions: more on point, better framed, and better phrased questions to yourself, to your core team, and, at times, to a larger community.

Better questions yield better results. Better questions point a group's thinking to where it needs to go. Simply put, well framed questions are critical to team focus and execution efficiency.

My hope is that this book enables you to practice more of the art that goes into asking good questions—the how.

**The first chapter** in the book helps you decide whether the question is worth posing to anyone beyond yourself. Often, the answer should be, "no." If the answer is "yes", this chapter, then, helps you develop a plan of action.

**The second chapter** helps you triangulate the question to ask what is happening in your world: a simple way for you to resolve what is topical and important.

**The third chapter** helps you make the leap from seeing what matters to posing the go-for-the-jugular question(s) around the subject: a mental leap.

**The last chapter** helps you structure or phrase of the question. Will people in the room understand what you are asking? Will they care?

Enlightened leadership—leadership that inspires and engages—rests on your ability to help people focus on the heart of the matter. Asking good questions serves as the means to that end. The goal of this book helps you achieve that goal in a clear, direct way.

CHAPTER 1

# Contemplate Intent and Game Plan

GREAT QUESTION!

- What does it mean to contemplate your intent and develop a game plan?
- Why is it important to consider your motivation and have a plan?
- How do you determine your intent?
- How to develop a game plan
- Story One
- Your Turn

# Contemplate Intent and Game Plan

## What does it mean to contemplate your intent and develop a game plan?

In this context, I encourage you to explore your motivation for taking on a collaborative challenge and create a plan that will enhance your chance for success.

You have an opportunity to apply a collaborative challenge as a means to engage your colleagues in resolving a critical business question with you. This question is, "Should you proceed?"

If you do proceed what points should you keep in mind to ensure you make productive use of your time, the time of the core team and the community at large?

From the moment you're seriously considering sponsoring a collaborative challenge or problem solving activity your questions to the people that you designate to support the activity, or core team should be:

**What critical business question can my community explore, and resolve together?**

**What does success look like from making this effort?**

Keep in mind that the challenge question will help the community surface the "how," and as the leader you provide the "why."

## Why is it important to consider your motivation and have a plan?

Your organization holds you accountable for the profit or loss of one of its brands, channels, or regions. Maybe you oversee the entire business as a whole.

It's a serious commitment. Do not allow the current fascination with collaboration, social media and the like get in the way of the fact that you will be having a business discussion, regardless of whether you're running a for-profit or non-profit business.

There will be challenges encountered along the way that will need to be addressed. Planning for these challenges as well as considering the productive use of resources, expected outcomes, and team member's personal energy on the subject of a collaborative challenge is paramount. The objective is to excite and engage verses disenchanting your business or department.

## PEOPLE ARE BUSY

Time is the biggest obstacle to getting people to consider a new challenge, use it wisely.

## IDEALLY

Each team member brings with them their perspective on what's important to the organization and what levers are worth pulling.

## How do you determine your intent?

*Are you serious about a Collaborative Challenge?*

Make an assessment of the potential of a collaborative challenge. Ask yourself, "is it worth it to pursue the challenge?"

Determine if the challenge focus is legitimate and not following a fad, by asking yourself the following questions:

- **Is it worth it to pursue the challenge? Is it a significant business issue?**
- **Is it a challenge/question you don't know the answer to?**
- **Are you prepared to go where the question takes you?**
- **Are you making space for exploring potential ideas?**
- **Do you have the vision and courage to accept where things might go?**
- **Are you willing to apply the time and resources required?**

If affirmative to the above then Go, if not then No-Go. No-Go is perfectly OK.

## How to develop a game plan

*Who should be on your core team?*

Typically a leader has 4–5 people they consult with on business issues.

These are people with experience in the areas to be explored. People with authority to make decisions in the domain of interest. People closest to the work being done.

It is assumed that the leader and his core team enjoys a reasonable grasp of challenges and opportunities and has the ability to transfer them to questions.

I recommend no substitutions, people without the authority or influence in the domain will most likely not be effective.

**CONSIDER
YOUR STAFF.**

Consider if the initiative
could serve as an
opportunity to develop your
high potential people.

**CONTRIBUTORS
NEED TO BE
INFORMED.**

Map out a communication
plan for your challenge
based on who needs to know
what and when. What are
you going to do with the
results? Set expectations
and timing.

*What roles should your core team members play?*
The campaign demands that certain people hold certain
roles. You have the opportunity to slot people into each role.

*Roles include:*

**Team Leader** – Head of P&L and/or Group Leader. As the
leader, focus your energy on helping the group articulate
the business problem—What is the challenge question?

**Facilitator and/or Enabler** – It is highly recommended that a
trained facilitator is familiar with this book's content
and leads the group activities in Chapters 2 through 4.

**Advisors and/or Collaborators** – Members of the core team.

**Stakeholders** – People who are promoting and supporting
the challenge.

**Challenge Community** – Group of people you will pose the
question to generate ideas.

*What support does your team need?*

**Get information from the stakeholders** – people promoting and supporting the challenge. Find out what their vision of the challenge may be.

**Make sure the stakeholders spend time** with you and your team refining this question.

**Stay engaged.** Do not delegate the formation of the challenge question.

**Do not assume** that your core team shares a clear understanding of the challenge that you want the community to address.

*What resources do you have to commit?*

Recognize that sponsoring a collaborative challenge means committing two types of resources:

1) Resource on the front end to properly frame and position the challenge

2) Resources to run the activity

You will personally need to commit time for planning and participating in the development of the question.

**REFRAIN FROM USING POWERPOINT PRESENTATIONS.**

They can curtail valuable engagement and dialogue.

**MEET WITH YOUR TEAM IN PERSON**

whenever and wherever possible. Face to face meetings increase the level of creativity and engagement.

*How do I launch the challenge question discussion?*

As the leader, you will be sponsoring a session that includes efforts outlined in Chapters 2 through 4 in one seamless conversation.

I highly recommend there be no pre-work or homework for the core team prior to the session. Team members should come with only their business savvy and an open mind. I find that too much preparation by the core team can limit free thinking and derail the discussion along predetermined agendas.

When you are prepared to launch, invite the core team to a facilitator lead brainstorming session that will determine where to focus the challenge (Chapter 2), what level of transformation or change you're seeking (Chapter 3) and how to form an effective challenge question (Chapter 4).

I suggest a personal letter inviting the core team to the session. Offered here is an example invitation letter.

Figure 1.1 Example letter to the Core Team

Hello,

Please reserve DAY, DATE, from 9–11 am in ROOM X
to participate in our challenge formation session. In this
session we will:

· Develop the critical business question on which we wish
  to engage the community

· Identify a cross section of the organization who could
  contribute diverse perspective

· Model a day in the life of an idea as it evolves and
  progresses within the community

· Review the level of commitment that people who will hold
  various roles within the community will need to make
  during the course of the challenge

We will use the outcome of the above work to develop
the challenge site and to help ensure the health of the
community, relative to our goals.

Please bring an open mind and your business savvy, only.


Regards,

John Leader

# Story One

*I once worked with a client who led the retail sales division in North America for a well-known brand in financial services. While successful, he was risk averse.*

*His risk aversion, honed to a fine point from having witnessed several missteps of his colleagues, caused him to want to test posing a challenge question to his associates, people who worked in the retail stores.*

*The company had recently moved offices. Although his organization in particular had a number of critical challenges facing them, he chose as a test to ask his people what they should name the new building. The organization had a long history of giving their buildings and conference rooms iconic names.*

*I observed as his engagement proceeded. On the one hand, the group did come up with a range of novel, compelling names for the building. He gained a diversity of perspective. On the other hand, his community and he, through various hallway conversations, began to ask, "Is this a good use of our time?"*

**His and my learning from this experience:** *time is ultimately our biggest competitor. Are we spending our time and personal energy, wisely?*

*Had he asked the questions "Is it worth it to pursue this challenge? Is it a significant enough business issue?" With an honest reflection on these two questions he may have concluded that asking his people to name the new building was a No-Go. Then he may have pursued a more relevant question to test the challenge question process.*

# Your Turn

What challenge is on your mind?

_____

_____

Is it worth it to pursue the challenge?

○ yes ○ no

Is it a significant business issue?

○ yes ○ no

Is it a challenge/question you don't know the answer to?

○ yes ○ no

Are you prepared to go where the question takes you?

○ yes ○ no

Are you making space for exploring potential ideas?

○ yes ○ no

Do you have the vision and courage to accept where things might go?

○ yes ○ no

Are you willing to apply the time and resources required?

○ yes ○ no

THOUGHTS

GREAT QUESTION!

"That's been one of my mantras—focus and simplicity. Simple can be harder than complex: You have to work hard to get your thinking clean to make it simple. But it's worth it in the end because once you get there, you can move mountains."

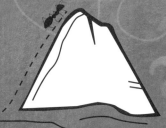

— STEVE JOBS

CHAPTER **2** Identifying the Challenge

- Introduction—Where do we focus our efforts?
- What is the Axis of Intent?
- Why is the Axis of Intent valuable?
- How to identify the Challenge using the Axis of Intent
- Discussing the Associate Experience
- Discussing the Customer Experience
- Discussing the Product/Service Offer
- Story Two
- Your Turn

# Identifying the Challenge

## Introduction—Where do we focus our efforts?

**Intent.** What does it mean to align intent of the business or organization with a collaborative challenge?

There are many different ways to express intent or identify a challenge. One method I find valuable for depicting the intent that drives many collaborative campaigns is the **Axis of Intent.**

The Axis of Intent has evolved through my own practice with clients to gain a broader perspective into what drives many sponsors and their campaign teams. In time, I began to sketch this newly found insight as a way to initiate dialogue around campaign formation.

It is important to note that the work outlined in this chapter as well as Chapters 3 and Chapters 4 are best performed in one continuous session with your core team.

## What is the Axis of Intent?

The Axis of Intent provides a framework for approaching the problem space through a simple visual for depicting strategic intent. It helps the team to be more conscious of their thinking when determining where to focus the challenge question.

## 2.1  Axis of Intent

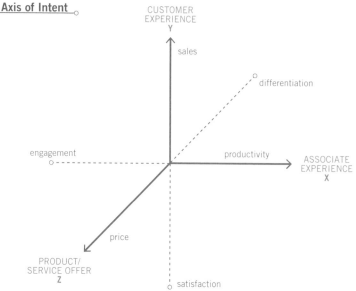

Figure 2.1 illustrates the Axis of Intent. The idea is that each axis relates to an essential area of focus for a business.

The X axis represents *Associate Experience*. The Y axis represents *Customer Experience*. The Z axis represents *The Offer*—the product or service being offered.

While the attributes for each axis presented here are not universal, the idea that every organization, profit or non-profit, has a set of financial metrics that define success or survival is universal.

The attributes presented here reflect my empirical understanding of what forms of intent drive innovation campaigns based on my experience. Invariably, I find when leaders are thinking about the business they are thinking along one of these axes.

Each axis is comprised of two components — "hard" metrics in the positive direction and "soft" metrics in the negative direction. "Hard" metrics imply financial results directly, where "soft" metrics do so indirectly.

In Figure 2.2, Associate Experience resolves to associate productivity for the hard metric and associate engagement for the soft.

**2.**2 | __Axis of Intent__

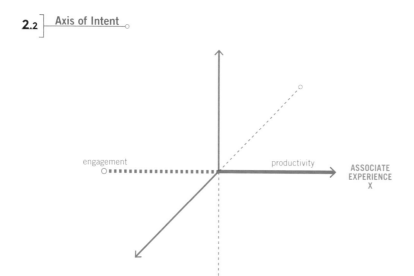

Figure 2.2 Associate Experience

Organizations can maximize productivity by introducing
new technologies or by offering opportunities for associates
to gain new competencies. Organizations may seek to
maximize associate engagement thus increasing associate
productivity.

**2.3** __Axis of Intent__

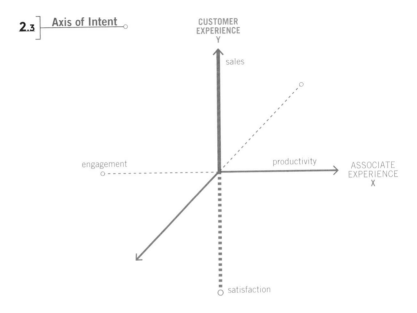

Figure 2.3 Customer Experience

In Figure 2.3, Customer Experience resolves to sales or revenue for the hard metric and customer satisfaction for the soft.

Organizations may seek to maximize sales or revenues directly by delivering new product and service innovations to the market. Or organizations may seek to maximize customer satisfaction thus increasing revenues they receive from customers.

**2.4** Axis of Intent

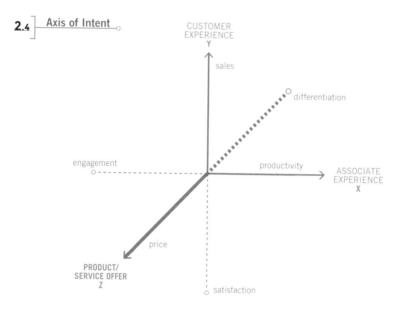

Figure 2.4 The Product/Service Offer resolves to price/promotion for the hard metric and differentiation for the soft.

## Why is the Axis of Intent valuable?

- Allows leaders to engage their organization—and, by extension, bring the strategic planning process alive.

- Offers simplicity in sharing organizational intent, and lends itself to visual storytelling on the value the organization aspires to deliver.

- Promotes conversation. People find value in the opportunity to engage in the challenge question of intent and resonate with the simple, visual approach.

- Inspires impromptu ideation sessions.

- Encourages leaders to think about the business multi-dimensionally.

## How to identify the Challenge using the Axis of Intent

This is the initial step for you and your core team to decide an effective challenge question. The leader and core team participates in a brainstorming session, led by the facilitator, using the Axis of Intent to arrive at a decision on where to focus together.

The focus area is selected by evaluating and defining business opportunities for associate experience, customer experience and the product/service offer using the Axis of Intent.

After the leader communicates the business objectives
and expectations, the facilitator starts the discussion by
conveying the concept of the Axis of Intent and then draws
and labels each of the three axes; X – Associate Experience,
Y – Customer Experience, and Z – Offer, Product/Service.

**2.5**  **Axis of Intent**

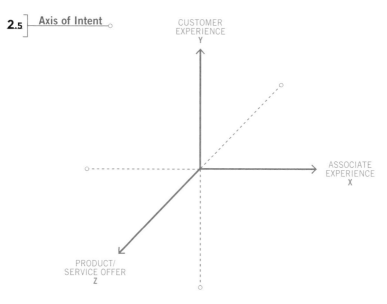

Figure 2.5 Initial Axis of Intent

Next, the facilitator initiates a discussion around each axis. The following is a suggested approach for each discussion.

## Discussing the Associate Experience

On the X axis, the facilitator initiates a discussion about opportunities pertaining to associate experience for both "hard" and "soft" metrics.

For example, the associate experience hard value might be Productivity. Here, the facilitator could ask questions like:

- **How much work do we get out of each associate?**
- **How might we improve the level of productivity per associate or work group?**

The soft value may be engagement, so the facilitator could ask questions like:

- **What can we do to increase associate engagement?**
- **How might we improve the associate experience?**

## Discussing the Customer Experience

On the Y axis, the facilitator initiates a discussion about opportunities pertaining to customer experience.

For example, the customer experience hard value might be share of wallet, or sales, and the facilitator could ask questions like:

- **How might we increase share of wallet through increased sales with the customers we have?**

The soft value might be customer satisfaction, the experience you deliver to your clients, customer, and consumers. The facilitator could ask questions like:

- **How might we deliver a more compelling customer experience?**

## Discussing the Product/Service Offer

And finally on the Z axis, the facilitator initiates a discussion about the offer, where the hard value might be price, promotion, or channel. The facilitator could ask questions like:

- **How might we price our offer?**

- **How might we promote our offer or bring it to market?**

Here the soft value might be differentiation, where questions might include:

- **What can we do or deliver that our competitors cannot?**

- **What makes you or your product more valuable in the eyes of the consumer?**

After completing the Axis of Intent, the team should utilize the process commensurate with your business practices to arrive at a decision of where to focus your challenge.

*I once worked with a client who prided herself on getting to the heart of the matter with her group by driving to the bottom line. She observed — and rightfully so, "No margin, no mission."*

*Her organization—a large, vertically integrated provider of healthcare — would be in no position to serve its population if they went bankrupt.*

*As a result, she focused on the "hard" or quantitative side of the three: pricing power, productivity, and sales.*

*She posed the question "How might we maximize the share of wallet for spending on healthcare?", the "hard" side of customer experience.*

*A member of her team felt engaged employees — nurses — were the foundation upon which his group would rise or fall, "soft" side of associate experience. In his mind, when the engaged employee delivered a quality patient experience the margins would follow.*

*His question was "How might we increase the level of satisfaction that nurses experience in delivering care?"*

*Others were compelled by questions around staff productivity, the "hard" side of associate experience.*

**2.6** Axis of Intent

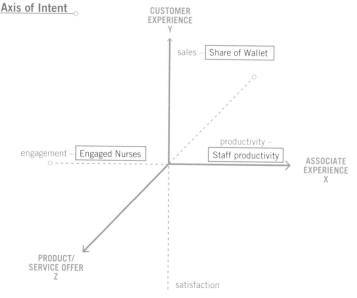

*In this case, The Axis of intent served as a visual way to have the conversation* that allowed them to arrive at a decision on where to focus. In the end they decided to start with "share of wallet" in the 3rd quarter, and "engaged nurses" in the 4th.

*Before using the Axis of Intent, the people in this story, absent a common point of reference, would often talk past one another. The leader found value in the Axis of Intent as a means to have more productive conversations on what mattered.*

YOUR TURN

**2.7** | Axis of Intent

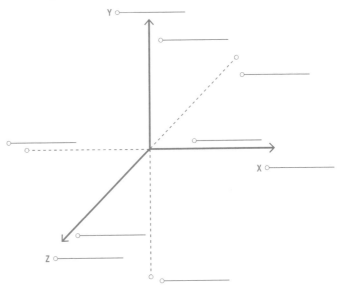

THOUGHTS

CHAPTER

# 3 Crafting the Challenge Question

# Crafting the Challenge Question

## Introduction

I would argue that there are an infinite number of "right" ways to ask the challenge question. The trick – secret handshake – is to align your questions with your business intent and to seek the right level of transformation that your team can manage.

## What is the Transformation Potential?

Challenge questions have "more" or "less" transformation potential.

People who sponsor a challenge expect certain outcomes. Some seek "low hanging fruit" or less transformation potential: small incremental forms of change that visibly improve existing processes and products. The organization can see immediate benefit.

Others, in contrast, seek "disruptive change" or high transformation potential. The ideas, when pursued with the requisite amounts of vision and courage, hold the potential to transform the organization's value chain and by extension, their market as a whole.

## Why is determining the Transformation Potential important when crafting the question?

How a question is composed affects how it will be perceived, understood, or reacted to.

Open-ended questions encourage creative thinking, out of the box ideas, and avoid leading a person or team to a specific answer. However, If the question is too open ended or too broad, it may lead to solutions unrelated to the challenge focus. Conversely, an overly restrictive, narrow question, may limit thought and creativity, so much so, that worthwhile ideas are not generated.

Striking a balance is key. Questions that are framed properly – that are neither too broad nor too narrow – increase the effectiveness of a question and maintain focus on the problem or challenge.

*The following is an example to explore the concept of transformation potential.*

Let us say you work for a company that makes hand soap. You wish to convene a community on a product improvement challenge. A perfectly fine basic challenge question might be:

**How might we, through washing, minimize the bacteria people have on their hands?**

This sort of question might lead to all sort of ideas around new product formulations and methods.

Consider by comparison, the following version:

**How might we minimize the rate of transfer of transmittable disease in the home?**

The second variation is not inherently superior to the first. It does, however, hold potential for greater transformation as shown in Figure 3.1.

**Why?** The second variation moves beyond the means (i.e. washing one's hands) to the ends (i.e. reduce transmission of disease).

**Context matters.** When your organization seeks "low hanging fruit" from the practice of collaborative innovation, dial back the transformation potential, or open-endedness of the question. Doing so keeps the community from swinging for the fences when your sponsor desires singles and doubles, to use a baseball analogy.

**GETTING TO THE HEART**

of the matter takes time and practice. Give the group space to explore the many angles and possibilities of the challenge question.

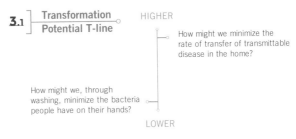

Figure 3.1 Illustration of ranking Transformation Potential

## How to craft the Challenge Question for the desired transformation?

With the challenge focus identified, the facilitator initiates a brainstorming session to generate a set of questions aligned with the challenge focus (identified using the Axis of Intent in Chapter 2: *Identifying the Challenge*).

I suggest the facilitator progressively moves through the following three steps, in a seamless flow providing little introduction of the process to follow. The idea here is not to introduce too many criteria or constraints which can limit free thinking:

**1 – Core team Initial brainstorming session.**

**2 – Open question exploration and transformation potential.**

**3 – Ranking the transformation potential and selecting the question.**

*1 – Core team initial brainstorm session*

First, the facilitator asks each team member to take 10 minutes and write out several questions (each using their own sheet of paper, note card or post-it) that one might ask to improve or enhance the challenge focus. Here you are looking for what is top of mind from the core team, not going for perfection.

After 10 minutes, the facilitator collects each participant's list and combines all of the team member's questions into one list on a white board for everyone to see using caution not to identify the source of the questions.

I find this brainstorming approach supports individual thought and reduces groupthink leading to higher participation of all team members.

Note: It is likely there will be similar versions of the same question. Working with the team, the facilitator can affinitize or consolidate the repetitive questions.

### 2 – Open Question exploration and transformation potential.

The next step is to explore the questions from the top of mind exercise through the lens of the transformation potential.

At this point, the facilitator introduces the concept of transformation potential, and then leads the group through an interactive brainstorming session using the top of mind results as a starting point.

This activity is organic and unscripted. The objective is to explore the meaning of each question and its contents. For instance, "customer" may appear in a question, which can spark a discussion around what customers is the team talking about. Or "price" may appear in a question and the team might evaluate what elements of price they are talking about. The goal during this discussion is to evolve the questions to different levels of transformation potential and to be more aligned with the intent or challenge focus.

**When facilitating sessions around this topic** – how to arrive at a question that best aligns with intent – I sometimes introduce the concept of anchor points to the core team as in Figure 3.2.

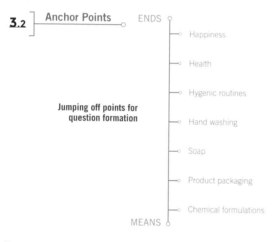

**3.2** — Anchor Points — ENDS
- Happiness
- Health
- Hygenic routines
- Hand washing
- Soap
- Product packaging
- Chemical formulations

**Jumping off points for question formation**

MEANS

Figure 3.2  Anchor points means of the inquiry to the ends of the inquiry.

To continue with the soap example, the facilitator might write on the whiteboard a list of words that move from the means of the inquiry (bottom of the list) to the ends of the inquiry (top of the list). That is, the soap company ultimately seeks to provide its consumers with greater happiness because they spend less time being sick from having caught a transmittable disease (e.g., disease caught by shaking unwashed hands).

The anchor points can serve as a way for the core team to begin to reform their questions.

Daniel Nolan, Principal Consultant at Denovo, offers another approach I find beneficial. Take the question at hand and ask "Why" a series of times. This can generate new questions, some more abstract and others more tactical.

For example starting with:

**"How might we build an efficient electric car?"**

*Why?*

**"Because we want a car that does not rely on fossil fuels."**

Phrasing the answer as a question yields,

**"How might we build a car not reliant on fossil fuels?"**

*Why?*

**"Because we want a car that burns clean, renewable energy."**

**Therefore, "How might we build a car that burns clean, renewable energy?"**

The last question is more abstract than the initial question. This will allow for ideas with more transformation potential.

Remember there is no one "right" way to form a challenge question. What is essential is that the question aligns with the strategic intent.

### 3 – Ranking the transformation potential and selecting the question

Now it's time to determine the relative transformation potential for each question.

The facilitator asks the core team to rank the transformation potential for each question on a scale from high to low. Typical group decision tools like "Dot Voting" can be used here, or other methods deemed appropriate by the facilitator.

With the questions "ranked", the team and/or leader can select a question that corresponds with the level of transformation they are prepared to take on.

I find there is typically one question that tends to resonate best with the group. The team should utilize a process commensurate with the business's practices to arrive at a decision on which question to take forward to the broader community.

# Story Three

*I once worked with a client who led a major line of business in the industrial chemicals industry. Her plants produced products in units of tons, loaded into tank cars.*

*She was a woman of integrity and someone who valued collaborative engagement. She also worked in a mature industry where pre-tax operating margins were forecast on the order of single basis points most quarters.*

*As a result, many of her inquiries to her organization were grounded in the reality of the here-and-now. She always sought "low hanging fruit." How might we improve an operating process? How might we stop doing one more thing that gets between us and our commercial clients?*

*Her reaction to the outcomes from these inquiries with her team was mixed. Many of the responses aligned with the day-to-day business at hand. She was looking for more transformational potential, but her questions did not inspire that.*

*There is an obligation on the leader to connect the dots and communicate their objective. Am I after significant transformation? Or am I after the low-hanging fruit?*

*Looking through the lens of transformation potential the leader and her team were able to think through the matter using of a simple tool that depicts the level of transformative*

*potential for each of the questions: the t-line. This led to a
question more aligned with where she wanted to go:*

*How might we increase the likelihood we become the
supplier of choice for our commercial clients?*

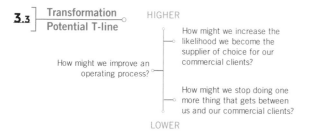

**3.3** Transformation
Potential T-line

HIGHER

How might we increase the
likelihood we become the
supplier of choice for our
commercial clients?

How might we improve an
operating process?

How might we stop doing one
more thing that gets between
us and our commercial clients?

LOWER

**Before being introduced to the t-line, this leader wrestled
with putting in context a question** *such as, "How might we
increase the likelihood we become the supplier of choice
for our commercial clients?", with a question such as,
"How might we stop doing one more thing that gets
between us and our commercial clients?". The leader found
value in being able to map the impact level of her intent
with her questions to the group.*

YOUR TURN

**3.4** Transformation Potential T-line

HIGHER

LOWER

THOUGHTS

GREAT QUESTION!

"The art of proposing a question must be held of higher value than solving it."

—GEORG CANTOR

# CHAPTER 4 Framing the Challenge Question

- What does it mean to frame the Challenge Question?
- Why is framing the Challenge Question important?
- How to frame the Challenge Question
- Story Four
- Your Turn

# Framing the Challenge Question

## What does it mean to frame the Challenge Question?

To get our heads around the concept of framing, I offer the late Arthur VanGundy's definition of framing questions to generate ideas.

*"Framing helps us to understand and to focus our thinking, thereby reducing uncertainty and enhancing human communication. An Ideal framing process helps us to deconstruct previously ambiguous situations, clarify and create focus so we can achieve our objectives."* [1]

**"A problem well-defined is half solved."**

**—John Dewey**

VanGundy's seminal work on the phrasing of challenge questions is effective and endures. The basic form of his phrasing follows:

How might we [increase/decrease] the [factor] in order to achieve [goal]?

[1] VanGundy, Arthur: *Getting to Innovation: How Asking the Right Questions Generates the Great Ideas Your Company Needs*, pp 11, 59.

## Why is framing the Challenge Question Important?

Format the question properly and you win more than half the battle in terms of ensuring your initiative succeeds from the start.

A well-framed question is critical to guiding the team in the right direction in a focused and efficient manner.

## How to frame the Challenge Question

With the question in hand, the facilitator introduces the question phrasing format as follows:

**How Might We [increase/decrease] the [factor] in order to achieve [goal]?**

If necessary, the facilitator reforms the question to comply with the *"How might we…"* phrasing.

The facilitator reworks the questions on the fly with the team to arrive at a well-framed question aligned with the business intent and the desired level of transformation. It may be necessary to go back to the focus area from the Axis of Intent exercise to ensure alignment.

*Be aware* – Sometimes there is buyer's remorse. After thinking about it you may determine that it is not the way you want to go.

*My guidance is that "buyer's remorse" is common* and to be expected after this sort of session. The day after, people left to their own thoughts and removed from the energy generated in the room together, and have time to think through more fully the implications of their decision.

*There's nothing wrong with having second thoughts.* Regrouping to do a mini "re-do" of the framing exercise makes perfect sense. Leaders over time come to bake-in time for self-reflection and expressions of reservations the day after the engagement.

*It is better to rethink and rework the challenge* up front before resources are expended on a challenge that does not serve the needs of the business.

With the question properly formulated, you are ready to pose the question to the broader community for idea generation.

**"Well Begun is half done."**
**—Aristotle**

# Story Four

*I once worked with a client who led business development for a consumer packaged goods company. It's likely that you have a few of their products in your home, today.*

*A strong leader, she was keenly interested in gathering the best insights from her group on how they might stay ahead of the game in a highly competitive market, where capturing another inch of shelf space in the retailer's stores made a lot of difference.*

*Interestingly, however, she struggled with the mechanics of asking a straight question.*

*Her invitations to engage appeared, for example, as a directive, "Please share your thoughts with me on keeping our clients."*

*Framing the question, as prescribed by Art Van Gundy, is a seemingly minor, yet important part of the process, including ensuring the question ends with a question mark.*

*Using the Van Gundy approach led her and her team to a more effective phrasing of the question:*

**How might we increase the likelihood that we retain client X in the coming year?**

**4.1** | Question Quality

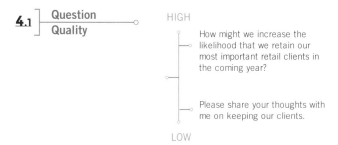

HIGH

How might we increase the likelihood that we retain our most important retail clients in the coming year?

Please share your thoughts with me on keeping our clients.

LOW

*This particular leader observed to me later that good technique around asking a question was like good technique around running a meeting: come prepared, have an agenda, etc.*

**Before she was introduced to this approach she had no fundamental technique to fashion an effective question.** *The leader found value in the Van Gundy phrasing as a means to ensure she was, in fact, asking a question.*

YOUR TURN

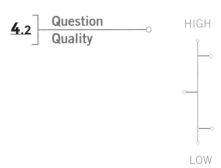

**4.2** Question
Quality

HIGH

LOW

THOUGHTS

# A Deeper Dive on Forming Questions

This book helps you to form compelling questions, readily. It is light on the why of the practice, by design.

Readers interested in a deeper dive into the topic will value the following resources.

**Art VanGundy** wrote the signature tome on question formation: *Getting to Innovation: How Asking the Right Questions Generates the Great Ideas Your Company Needs*. Of particular interest is the concept of question banks: the means by which an organization creates a repository of critical questions to pose about the business, tied to a holistic look at the business' goals.

**Juanita Brown and David Isaacs** wrote the signature tome on convening people to form and pursue questions: *The World Cafe Book: Shaping Our Futures through Conversations that Matter*. Of particular interest is the means by which people who sponsor inquiries (i.e., the readers of this book) can increase the likelihood of success by creating the right setting and the right tone.

**Lastly, the International Association of Facilitators (IFA)** serves as the de facto community of practice, worldwide, for people who convene others in inquiry. Annual membership to the IFA is a nominal USD 200, which gives you access to fellow practitioners and their many resources.

# Acknowledgements

Every organization, with luck, employs people with the courage, vision, and integrity to pose the critical question. The following people, through our dialogue on question formation, offered me material support in developing this book. Paul Lesner and Chuck Whitlock at Duke Energy. Mark Polson and Shruti Padilla at The Estee Lauder Companies. Rick Smyers and Deb Bovino at Fidelity Investments. Harry Brandicourt, Mike Crawford, and Leo Smith at Fifth Third Bank. Adryanna Sutherland at Gyro. Laurie Heltsley (retired) and Suna Polat (retired) at The Procter & Gamble Company. Therese Steiner at RELX Group. Tex Texeira at Sprint Corporation.

Jon and Rondi Tschopp at Five Visual applied their formidable listening and design skills to turn my very early, "How might we write a book about questions?" question into a quality work.

My colleagues at Spigit serve as a continual, ready source of inspiration, as we work to make real the means by which organizations thrive in the Digital Age.

Doug Collins serves as an innovation management consultant. He engages organizations such as The Estee Lauder Companies, Fidelity Investments, Intel Corporation, Johnson & Johnson, and The Procter & Gamble Company in navigating the fuzzy front end of innovation.

Doug develops approaches, creates forums, and structures engagements whereby people can convene to explore the critical questions facing the enterprise. He helps people assign economic value to the ideas and to the collaboration that result.

As an author, Doug explores ways in which people can apply the practice of collaborative innovation in his series Innovation Architecture: A New Blueprint for Engaging People through Collaborative Innovation.

His bi-weekly column appears in the publication Innovation Management. Doug serves on the board of advisors for Frost & Sullivan's Global community of Growth, Innovation and Leadership (GIL).

Doug works as senior practice leader and Vice President, Innovation Architecture, at social innovation company Spigit, part of Mindjet, Inc. He focuses on helping clients realize their potential for leadership by pursuing and perfecting their practice of collaborative innovation.

Doug and his family live in Cincinnati, Ohio.

GREAT QUESTION!